T0413701

A-**MAZE**-ING
ADVENTURES

A-**MAZE**-ING ADVENTURES
IN **AFRICA** AND **EUROPE**

Lisa Regan

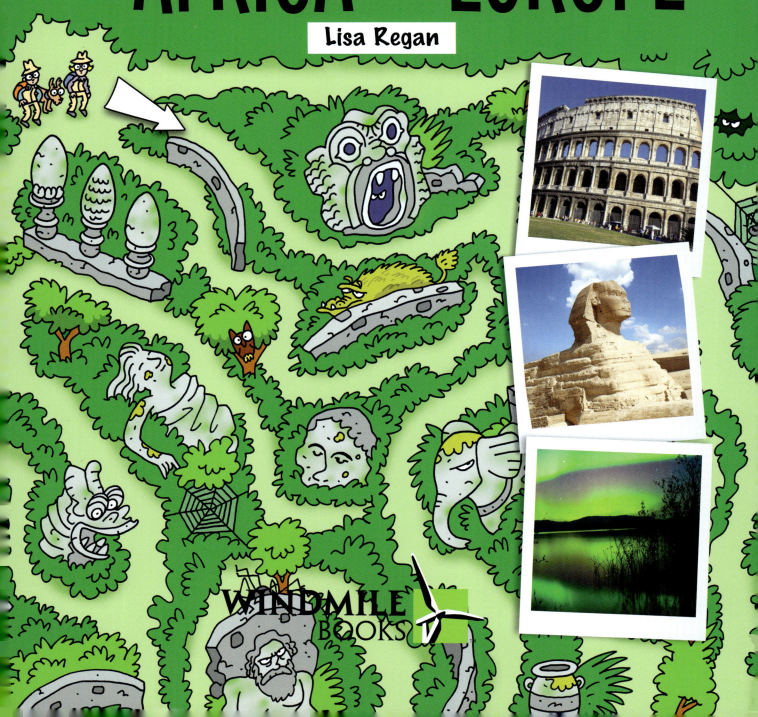

WINDMILL
BOOKS

Are you ready... for the adventure of a lifetime?

Join us, Max, Millie, and our pet dog, Mojo, on a trip to see amazing and exciting sights! Everywhere we go, we'll need your help. Use your finger to help us solve the tricky mazes. Along the way, we'll find hidden objects and learn some fascinating facts. We're going to take lots of photographs and make notes as we go.

Published in 2021 by Windmill Books,
an Imprint of Rosen Publishing
29 East 21st Street, New York, NY 10010

Copyright © Arcturus Holdings Ltd, 2021

Cataloging-in-Publication Data

Names: Regan, Lisa.
Title: A-maze-ing adventures in Africa and
Europe / Lisa Regan
Description: New York : Windmill Books, 2021.
| Series: A-maze-ing adventures | Includes
glossary and index.
Identifiers: ISBN 9781499485455 (pbk.) |
ISBN 9781499485479 (library bound) | ISBN
9781499485462 (6 pack) | ISBN 9781499485486
(ebook)
Subjects: LCSH: Maze puzzles--Juvenile literature.
| Africa--Juvenile literature. | Europe--Juvenile
literature.
Classification: LCC GV1507.M3 P484 2021 | DDC
793.73'8--dc23

Manufactured in the United States of America

CPSIA Compliance Information: Batch BS20WM: For Further Information contact Rosen Publishing, New York, New York at 1-800-237-9932

Find us on

Contents

Ted the ginger cat is going to tag along. He goes everywhere we go, but he's very shy, so he'll be hiding most of the time. See if you can find him in each maze!

Welcome to EUROPE

We're so excited! Our adventure starts in chilly Norway, where we hope to see the Northern Lights. Then we'll take in some history in London, the United Kingdom, and call in at the famous Berlin Zoo in Germany. There's more sightseeing and history at the Eiffel Tower in Paris and farther south in Italy's capital city: majestic Rome.

NORTH AMERICA

SOUTH AMERICA

EUROPE

ASIA

AFRICA

AUSTRALASIA

Northern Lights

Wow! Today we are visiting Norway to see the Northern Lights. These swirling patterns of light in the night sky are totally amazing.

FACT FILE

COUNTRY: Norway
CONTINENT: Europe
CAPITAL CITY: Oslo

The Northern Lights are created by electrically charged particles bumping together in the atmosphere. They can often be seen in northern Norway between late autumn and early spring. Norway is in part of Europe called Scandinavia. It stretches from its capital, Oslo, in the south, to the far north in the Arctic. Its coastline is packed with stunning fjords: long, narrow valleys with steep sides, created by glaciers.

Some fjords have coral reefs at the bottom!

reindeer, or caribou

Show Max and Millie how to ski through the slopes of the maze to reach the cozy log cabin.

START

END

On Guard

We're brushing up on our history today! The Tower of London is a historic castle on the banks of the River Thames. We can't wait to take a look inside!

FACT FILE

COUNTRY: United Kingdom
CONTINENT: Europe
CAPITAL CITY: London

Today, the Tower of London is home to hundreds of precious objects such as crowns, swords, bracelets, rings, and royal robes. In past centuries, it was a prison, and many people, including kings and queens, were thrown in the dungeons here. The Tower was built as a castle for William the Conqueror after he became king of England in 1066. It has also been used as a royal zoo!

The guards at the Tower wear special uniforms and are nicknamed Beefeaters.

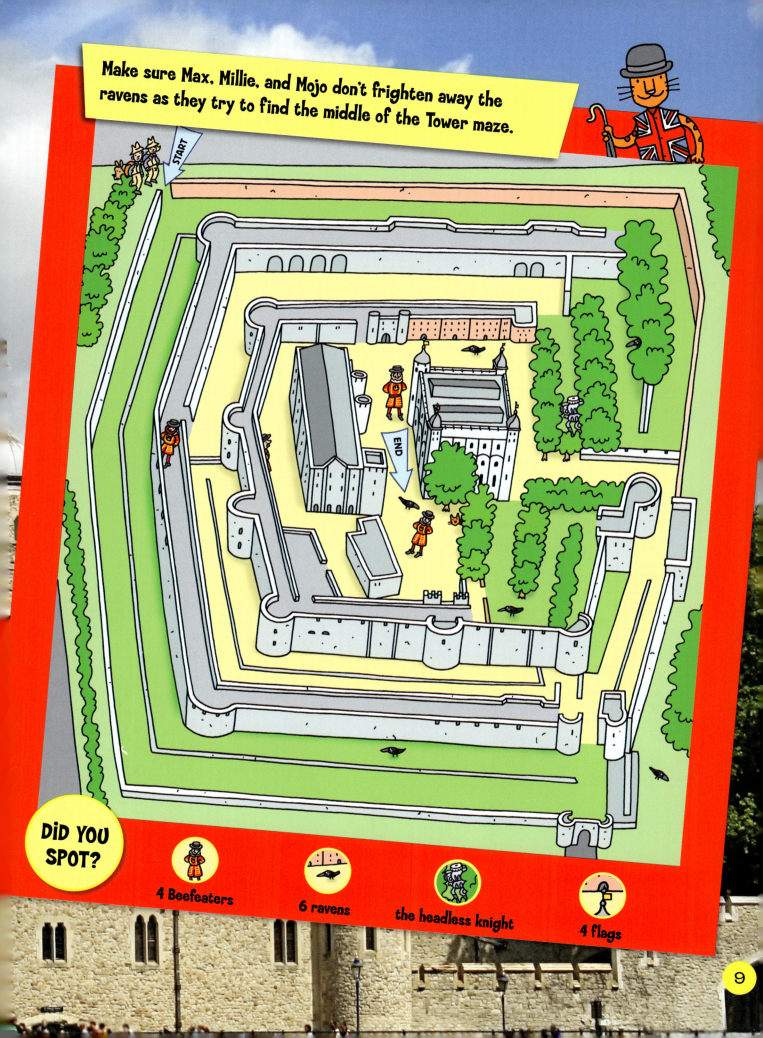

Make sure Max, Millie, and Mojo don't frighten away the ravens as they try to find the middle of the Tower maze.

START

END

DID YOU SPOT?

4 Beefeaters

6 ravens

the headless knight

4 flags

A Day at the Zoo

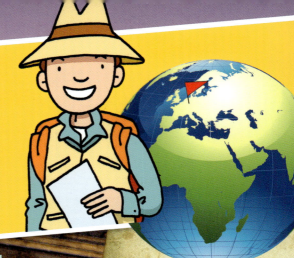

Berlin Zoo is the oldest zoo in Germany. No dogs are allowed in, but Mojo is happy seeing Berlin's other sights while he waits!

FACT FILE

COUNTRY: Germany
CONTINENT: Europe
CAPITAL CITY: Berlin

Berlin Zoo opened in 1844 but was destroyed during World War II, along with many of Berlin's historic buildings. The impressive Brandenburg Gate (pictured) was also damaged, but it was restored at the start of the 21st century. After World War II, Germany was split into two countries, East Germany and West Germany. Berlin was divided for around 30 years by the Berlin Wall, but today it is one busy, thriving, united city.

The Berlin Wall, which divided the city in two, was built in 1961.

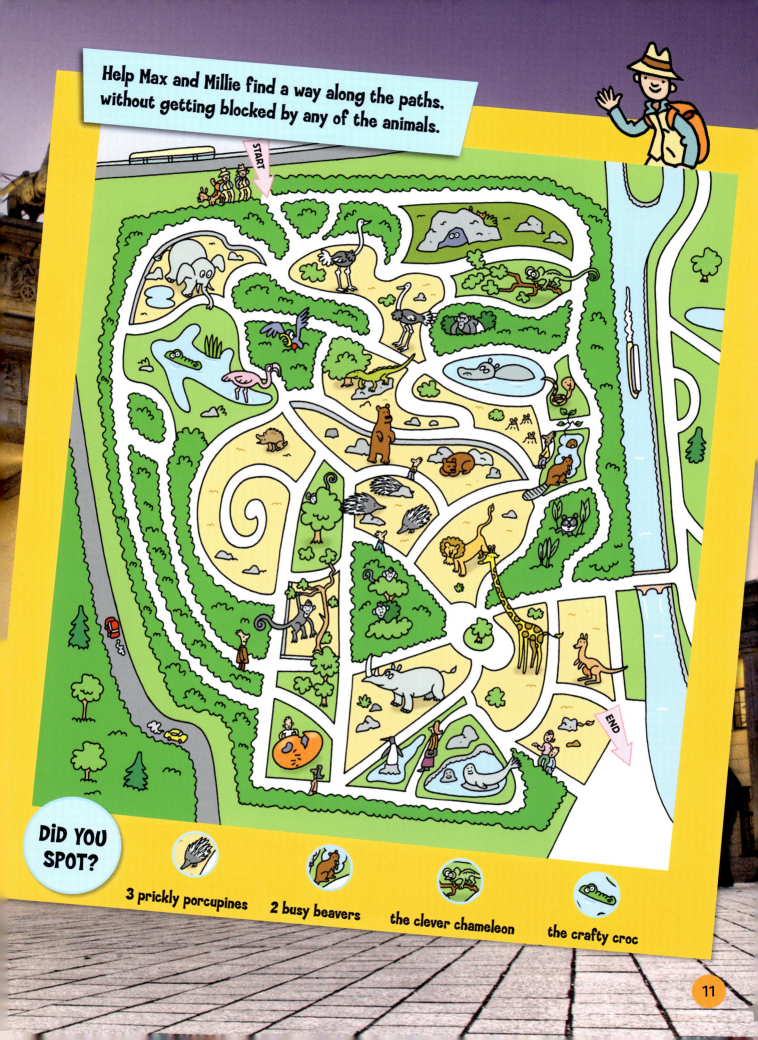

Help Max and Millie find a way along the paths, without getting blocked by any of the animals.

START

END

DID YOU SPOT?

3 prickly porcupines

2 busy beavers

the clever chameleon

the crafty croc

11

Bonjour!

We are at one of the most famous sights in the world! The Eiffel Tower in Paris is made of iron, and we are taking an elevator almost to the top!

FACT FILE

COUNTRY: France
CONTINENT: Europe
CAPITAL CITY: Paris

Les Invalides

The Eiffel Tower was built in 1889 as a dramatic entrance archway for the World's Fair held in Paris. At the time, it was the world's tallest structure. It was meant to be pulled down after 20 years, but it was kept standing and has now had over 250 million visitors! Paris is full of historic sights, such as Les Invalides, home of the tomb of the great military leader Napoleon Bonaparte. Paris is the capital of France, the largest country in Western Europe.

The Arc de Triomphe commemorates French soldiers.

12

Our friends have seen the sights – now they want to come down! Help them to the bottom of the tower.

START

END

Roman Ruins

FACT FILE

COUNTRY: Italy
CONTINENT: Europe
CAPITAL CITY: Rome

Rome is Italy's largest city and is full of historical sites. In ancient times, it became the center of an enormous empire called the Roman Empire, which covered huge parts of Africa and Europe. The Colosseum was built between 72 and 81 CE as a giant stadium where around 50,000 people could watch gladiators fighting. Amazingly, it could even be filled with water to show pretend sea battles!

The Trevi Fountain took 30 years to complete.

Can you help Max, Millie, and Mojo through the Park of the Monsters in Bomarzo?

START

END

DID YOU SPOT?

6 owls

3 spiders' webs

the hairy beast

2 mysterious monsters

Welcome to
AFRICA

Africa is the world's second-largest continent. We're starting in Egypt in the far north, to see the pyramids and the River Nile. We plan to follow the Nile south to Uganda, to see gorillas in the wild. Then it's on to Tanzania, where it's all about the wildlife, and Namibia, with sand dunes as well as safaris! Finally, we're staying in South Africa, to see its busy cities and cool coastlines. Are you ready for the trip?

NORTH AMERICA

SOUTH AMERICA

EUROPE

ASIA

AFRICA

AUSTRALASIA

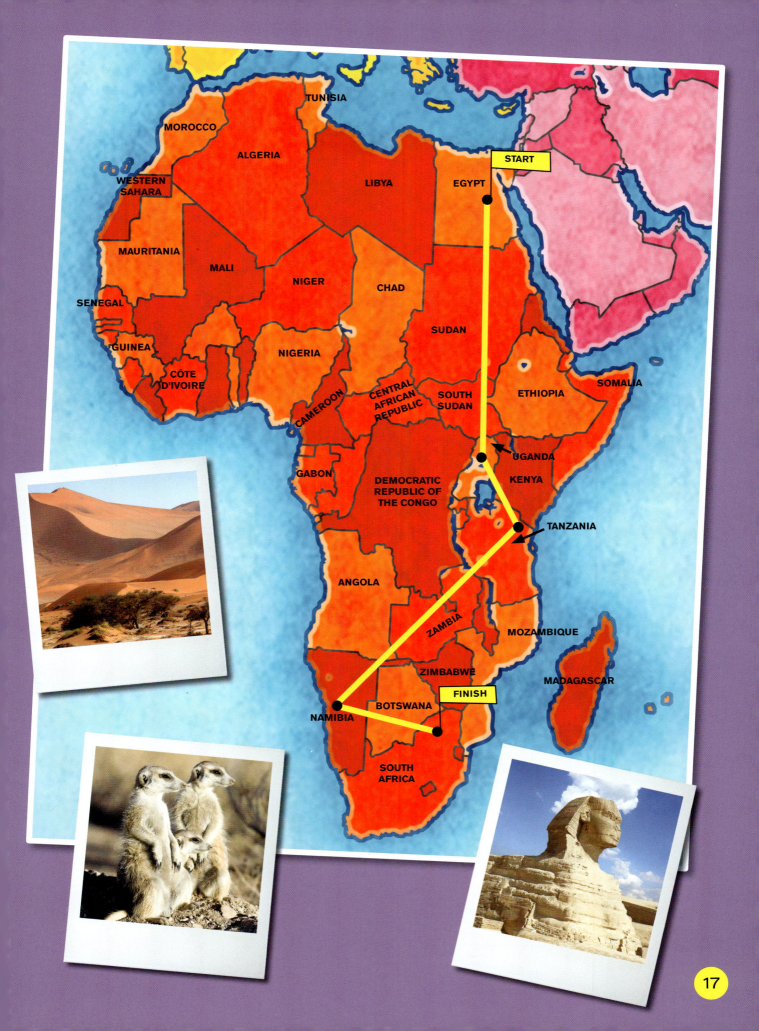

Pyramid Quest

There used to be a list of Seven Wonders of the Ancient World. Today, the only one left standing is the Great Pyramid of Giza in Egypt. We can't believe how old it is!

Egypt is an amazing country in the far north of Africa. Large parts of it are desert with extremely high sand dunes. Most people in Egypt live in the narrow Nile Valley, where the land is fit for farming and building. The ancient rulers, called pharaohs, built extravagant burial sites along the River Nile. Pharaoh Khufu was buried in the Great Pyramid over 4,500 years ago.

The Sphinx is the world's biggest single-stone statue.

camel – ship of the desert

The Great Pyramid's smooth white covering no longer exists, so it's a bumpy path to the top these days!

END

START

DID YOU SPOT?

the desert dog

the mischievous mouse

the slithering snake

3 sneaky scorpions

Gorilla Safari

If you want to see the endangered mountain gorilla, the central African rain forest is the place to go. We are trekking through Uganda, hoping to catch a glimpse of these mighty mammals.

FACT FILE

COUNTRY: Uganda
CONTINENT: Africa
CAPITAL CITY: Kampala

Some of the world's last remaining mountain gorillas live in the Bwindi Impenetrable Forest in Uganda. The rain forest lies along the edge of the East African rift valley, where Earth's crust is splitting apart. The River Nile flows north from Lake Victoria, eventually joining the Mediterranean Sea. On its journey, the Nile bursts through a tiny gap in the rocks to form the Murchison Falls (shown at the right) in northern Uganda.

There are only around 700 mountain gorillas left in the wild today.

Shh! Can you work your way through the forest undergrowth without disturbing the sleeping gorillas?

START

END

DID YOU SPOT?

2 okapis

Gerald the giraffe

the sleepiest gorilla

the baby gorilla

Tanzania Trek

We're going on a very long walk! First, we are off to see the wildlife in the national parks, followed by climbing Mount Kilimanjaro, the highest mountain in Africa!

FACT FILE

COUNTRY: Tanzania
CONTINENT: Africa
CAPITAL CITY: Dodoma

Tanzanite is blue but can look violet or reddish-brown under different lights.

Tanzania is on the eastern coast of Africa, and its people are mostly farmers, although the country is also Africa's third-largest producer of gold. It has its own precious gemstone, tanzanite, found nowhere else in the world. Each year thousands of tourists visit Tanzania's national parks. Serengeti National Park is home to Africa's "Big Five": lions, leopards, elephants, rhinoceroses, and buffalo.

Before they take on the mountain, the gang is off on safari. Help them on their dusty drive!

START

END

DID YOU SPOT?

4 wary warthogs

3 shy snakes

3 enormous elephants

the sleeping lion

Red Desert

The Namib Desert is so beautiful! The red dunes are caused by iron in the sand. You could almost imagine that you are walking on Mars!

FACT FILE

COUNTRY: Namibia
CONTINENT: Africa
CAPITAL CITY: Windhoek

Look! It's an impala!

Many of Namibia's sand dunes are pink or orange, but the oldest ones are red. They are some of the highest dunes in the world. Namibia is in southern Africa and contains two deserts: the Namib and the Kalahari. It is also home to Etosha National Park, where you can see a variety of wildlife, including giraffes, meerkats, and several types of antelope, such as impalas.

A group of meerkats is called a mob.

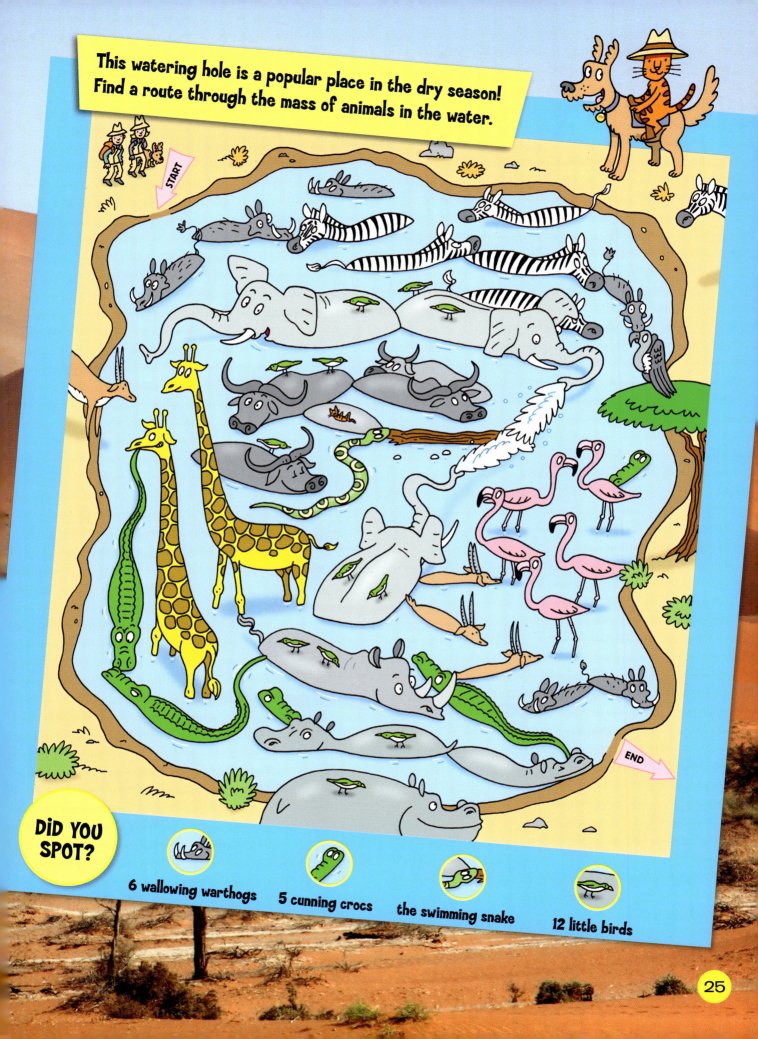

This watering hole is a popular place in the dry season! Find a route through the mass of animals in the water.

START

END

DID YOU SPOT?

6 wallowing warthogs   5 cunning crocs   the swimming snake   12 little birds

25

Southern Tip

We are down at the southernmost point of Africa: a land of gold, diamonds, busy cities, and wonderful wildlife. Let's go!

FACT FILE

COUNTRY: South Africa
CONTINENT: Africa
CAPITAL CITY: Pretoria

There's so much to see in South Africa! It has some of Africa's best-known game reserves, where wild animals roam and hunt but remain protected from poachers. It also has thousands of miles of coastline, with regular visits from sharks, whales, and penguins. Its largest cities are Johannesburg, incorporating the famous township of Soweto, and Cape Town, overlooked by the flat-topped Table Mountain.

Cape Town nestles at the foot of Table Mountain.

The trio has been staying at the luxurious Palace of the Lost City Hotel! Help them find their way out of the resort.

END

START

DID YOU SPOT?

5 perky parrots

4 slithery snakes

3 funny monkeys

2 slinking leopards

Answers

6–7   Northern Lights

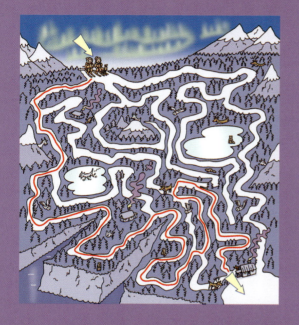

8–9   On Guard

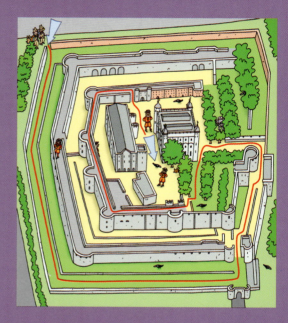

10–11   A Day at the Zoo

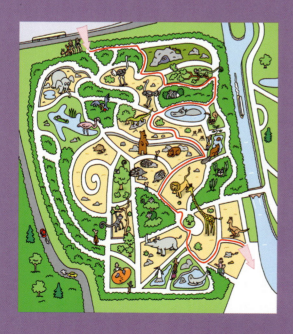

12–13   Bonjour!

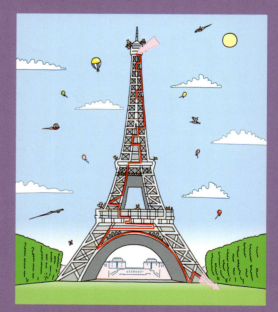

14–15   Roman Ruins

18–19   Pyramid Quest

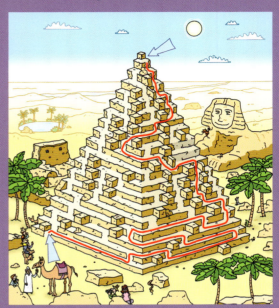

20–21   Gorilla Safari

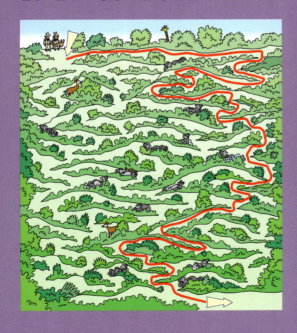

22–23   Tanzania Trek

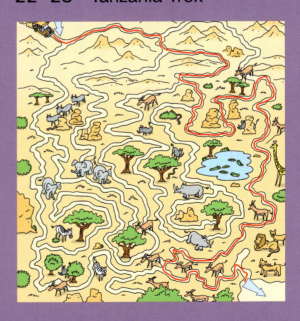

Glossary

atmosphere The gases that surround a planet.

commemorate To do or produce something to remember an event or person by.

continent Any of the world's seven main landmasses.

empire A group of states or countries ruled over by one leader.

gladiators In ancient Rome, men trained to fight other men or animals in the great arena.

Scandinavia Denmark, Norway, and Sweden.

tomb A building where someone's body is kept after they have died.

World War II The war of 1939 to 1945 fought between the Axis Powers (Germany, Italy, and Japan) and the Allies (Great Britain, the United States, and the Soviet Union).

Further Information

Books

Children's Picture Atlas Usborne, 2003

Europe / Africa (Go Exploring! Continents and Oceans) by Steffi Cavel-Clarke, BookLife Publishing, 2017

Mapping Europe / Africa (Close-Up Continents) by Paul Rockett, Franklin Watts, 2016

The Travel Book: A Journey Through Every Country in the World Lonely Planet Kids, 2017

Websites

www.google.com/earth

Explore the world in stunning satellite imagery.

www.natgeokids.com/za/category/discover/geography

National Geographic Kids has a wealth of information on animals and countries.

Publisher's note to educators and parents: Our editors have carefully reviewed these websites to ensure that they are suitable for students. Many websites change frequently, however, and we cannot guarantee that a site's future contents will continue to meet our high standards of quality and educational value. Be advised that students should be closely supervised whenever they access the Internet.

Index